MINERALS, ROCKS AND FOSSILS

This I-SPY book belongs to:______________

Introduction

The materials from which everything in the world, including humans, are made come from the Earth. The buildings in which we live, work, or go to school are built mostly from metal, bricks, or stone. Iron is sometimes used for the support structure, bricks for the walls, and stone may give the finish to the floors or the outside facing. These materials are the products of human skills and enterprise but, originally, they come from some of the natural substances from which our planet, Earth, is made. The Moon and the other planets in our solar system are also built of rocks and minerals. Sand and gravel are examples of rocks formed at the surface of the Earth. Some rocks are laid down in the seas and oceans while others are produced from the hot mineral melts that occur at great depths below the surface of the earth.

Proof of the great processes at work in our planet's inner layers is found in areas of volcanic activity. Hot, molten rocks may pour out forming rivers of lava glowing orange-red before cooling and solidifying. Fragments of lava are often blasted skywards falling as a cindery rubble. Evidence of ancient volcanic activity can be found in many areas, and the rocks themselves are often used in the construction of public buildings because, when cut and polished, they can be very beautiful. Weathering, through rain, wind, ice, or just the heat of the sun, will gradually break rocks down into smaller and smaller fragments. The minerals that once formed a lava may become the new constituents of a sand or gravel. In the seas and oceans, animals and plants build skeletons of calcite or silica, two of the most abundant minerals.

The first skeletons are recorded from rocks over 600 million years old although simple plants first built robust, layered structures about 3.5 billion years ago. The rocks around us show the history of our planet from its origin 4.6 billion years ago to the present day. Remember, everything you see has either been made, or formed, from materials found only on this earth.

How to use your I-SPY book

Many of the minerals, rocks, and fossils shown in this I-Spy book are quite easy to find in the fields, or on buildings, or as jewellery. Others are rare and you will be able to see them only in museums or other collections. This book is divided into three main sections but remember that rocks are just aggregates of minerals. When you study a specimen, try to identify the individual minerals or fossils within it. You need 1000 points to send off for your I-Spy certificate (see page 64) but that is not too difficult because there are masses of points in every book. As you make each I-Spy, write your score in the box and, where there is a question, double your score if you can answer it. Check your answer against the correct one on page 63.

DIAMOND

Natural form: octahedral, eight-sided, crystals with curved faces. Flat grains.

Hardness: hardest natural substance known.

Colour: top quality are colourless, yellowish, bluish. Can be red, brown or black.

Found: in kimberlite rock filling ancient vertical pipes of great depth. Detrital in gem gravels.

Uses: jewellery, cutting tools, diamond drills.

I-SPY points: 50

Date: ____________

SULPHUR

Natural form: tabular crystals or crystals resembling pyramids joined base to base.

Hardness: can be scratched with a finger nail.

Colour: bright yellow, sometimes with a brown tinge; white streak; resin-like lustre.

Found: in volcanic areas as masses round vents and in fractures in limestones.

Uses: in the manufacture of sulphuric acid, matches, and in some insecticides.

I-SPY points: 20

Date: ____________

PYRITE

Natural form: cubic crystals,
Hardness: difficult to scratch with a knife; will mark glass.
Colour: brassy or golden yellow; black streak; metallic lustre.
Found: in association with igneous rocks; in black shales as cubes or nodules; or in mineral veins; widespread. Pyrite fractures easily and weathers quickly.
Uses: in the manufacture of sulphuric acid; ornamental.

Because it resembles a precious metal, what name is sometimes given to pyrite?

I-SPY points: 10, double with answer

Date: ____________

GRAPHITE

Natural form: massive lumps or tabular crystals.
Hardness: may be marked with a finger nail.
Colour: black; black streak; dull, metallic sheen.
Found: in rocks changed by temperature and/or pressure, such as in schists, and in pegmatite veins.
Uses: in making pencils and in the electricity industry.

Graphite is sometimes wrongly given the name of a heavy metal. Which metal?

I-SPY points: 30, double with answer

Date: ____________

SPHALERITE

Natural form: as four-sided crystals or complex variations. Also massive part-crystalline or even fibrous.
Hardness: easily scratched by pocket knife, but it will scratch a copper coin.
Colour: resinous yellow, through various shades of translucent or even opaque brown.
Found: in metamorphic deposits and veins with white calcite, grey galena and sometime pyrite.
Uses: the most valuable ore of zinc.

I-SPY points: 40

Date: ____________

ORPIMENT

Natural form: as columnar masses and banded forms.
Hardness: very soft – easily scratched by finger nail. Poisonous – contains arsenic.
Colour: lemon yellow with streaks of red, sometime translucent on edges.
Found: in association with the red mineral realgar in limestone and veins rich in arsenic.
Uses: as a pigment and in the treatment of animal skins.

I-SPY points: 40

Date: ____________

HAEMATITE

Natural form: tabular crystals, rose-like growths and domed masses (kidney ore).
Hardness: can be marked with a knife but will just scratch glass.
Colour: reddish black, steel grey, black; dark- red streak; metallic lustre.
Found: usually in sandstones and limestones affected by mineral-rich fluids; widespread.
Uses: an important iron ore, and in stains and pigments.

I-SPY points: 20

Date: ____________

GALENA

Natural form: cubic; may also be massive or granular.
Hardness: can be scratched with a knife.
Colour: dull lead grey; dull grey streak; metallic lustre.
Found: in veins and in sedimentary rocks that have been soaked with hot fluids rising from the inner Earth, in areas such as south-west England, the Pennines and Scotland.
Uses: an important lead ore.

I-SPY points: 20

Date: ____________

CASSITERITE

Natural form: pyramid-like crystals or massive ore deposit.
Hardness: will scratch glass.
Colour: black or red-brown; white-grey streak; slightly metallic sheen.
Found: associated with pegmatite veins and near granite intrusions; in south-west England, for example.
Uses: an important ore of tin; also known as tinstone.

I-SPY points: 40

Date: ____________

CORUNDUM

Natural form: barrel-shaped, pyramid-like, or tabular crystals.
Hardness: very hard, will scratch glass.
Colour: brown to blue-grey; ruby and sapphire (varieties) are red and blue respectively; glassy lustre.
Found: in pegmatite veins and metamorphic rocks; gems may occur in river or stream deposits; rare.
Uses: as an abrasive; gemstones in jewellery.

I-SPY points: 50

Date: ____________

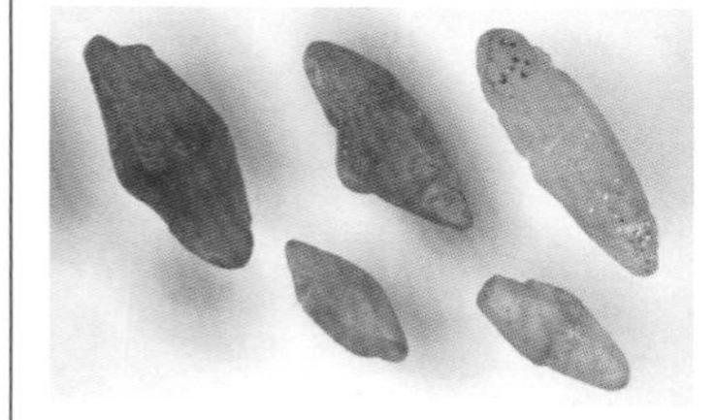

RUBY

Natural form: barrel shaped prisms, often tapering toward the ends.
Hardness: second to diamond, by which it can be scratched. Can scratch steel.
Colour: delicate to deep transparent red.
Found: in nepheline syenite pegmatites (rocks containing large crystals). Detrital in gem gravels in streams.
Uses: as a gemstone in jewellery.

I-SPY points: 15

Date:

SAPPHIRE

Natural form: barrel shaped prisms, often tapering toward the ends.
Hardness: second to diamond, by which it can be scratched. Can scratch steel.
Colour: delicate to deep transparent blue.
Found: in nepheline syenite pegmatites (rocks containing large crystals). Detrital in gem gravels in streams.
Uses: much prized as a gemstone for jewellery.

I-SPY points: 15

Date:

BAUXITE

Natural form: earthy, massive or concretionary masses.
Hardness: because of its generally earthy and colloidal nature it does not have a recognised hardness.
Colour: white when pure to brick-red to ochreous yellow
Found: bauxite is a secondary hydroxide of aluminium typical of tropical weathering of rocks rich in aluminium.
Uses: valuable ore of aluminium.

I-SPY points: 30

Date: ____________

MAGNETITE

Natural form: massive, or eight sided or cubic crystals and often granular.
Hardness: just scratched by pocket knife or steel file.
Colour: black. Silvery black due to reflections from surface.
Found: common as small grains in all igneous rocks and metamorphic rocks.
Uses: because it is strongly magnetic, it was used as a compass (lodestone) in early times. Of economic value as iron ore.

I-SPY points: 45

Date: ____________

HALITE

Natural form: cubes and as massive deposits of rock salt.
Hardness: can just be scratched with a finger nail.
Colour: colourless, white, and yellow, sometimes red and blue; white streak; glassy lustre.
Found: associated with the evaporation of salt-water brines, found as layered deposits; in the English Midlands, for example.
Uses: in the manufacture of hydrochloric acid and in foods.

I-SPY points: 30

Date:

CALCITE

Natural form: prisms, rhomb-like crystals, and fibres. Dog-tooth spar is a very common form.
Hardness: easily scratched with a knife.
Colour: colourless or white if pure, various colours if stained; white streak; glassy lustre.
Found: as crystals in veins, but is an important mineral in limestones and as a cement; widespread.
Uses: in the cement industry; smelting; fertilizers.

I-SPY points: 10

Date:

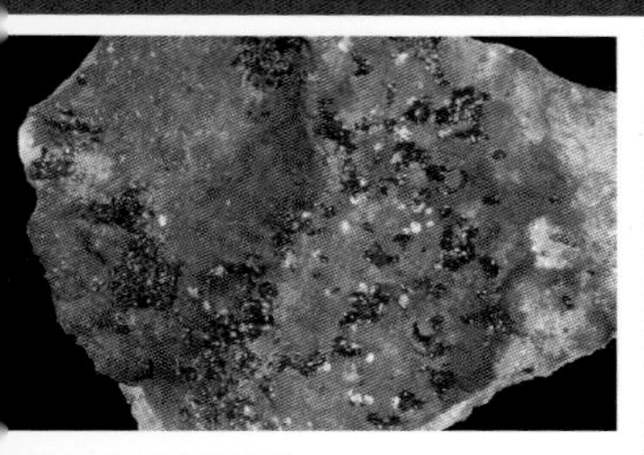

AZURITE

Natural form: as tabular or short prismatic crystals. Also massive radiating clusters and soil-like masses.
Hardness: easily scratched by a pocket knife
Colour: vivid azure blue transparent to translucent crystals.
Found: often associated with its sister copper mineral – green malachite. Occurs in the upper, near surface, zones of copper deposits
Uses: as an ore of copper. Good crystals are prized by mineral collectors.

I-SPY points: 40

Date: ____________

FLUORITE

Natural form: mostly cubes but sometimes rhomb-like.
Hardness: can be scratched with a knife.
Colour: yellow, blue, green, purple, and even black; white streak; glassy lustre.
Found: in mineral veins in limestone areas associated with quartz, barytes, and galena; such as the Pennines and the Lake District.
Uses: in smelting; ornamental.

I-SPY points: 30

Date: ____________

SIDERITE

Natural form: rhomb-like crystals with curved faces; may also be fibrous or massive.
Hardness: can be scratched with a knife.
Colour: grey, yellow- brown; white streak; glassy lustre.
Found: as clay ironstone and in veins, in areas such as the Midlands and Pennines.
Uses: iron ore.

I-SPY points: 40

Date:

DOLOMITE

Natural form: rhomb-like crystals with curved faces, or as a rock-forming mineral.
Hardness: can be scratched with a knife.
Colour: colourless, white, pink, or yellow-brown; white streak; pearly to glassy lustre.
Found: widespread as a rock-forming mineral.
Uses: building stone and for making furnace bricks.

Where are the Dolomite Mountains?

I-SPY points: 10, double with answer

Date:

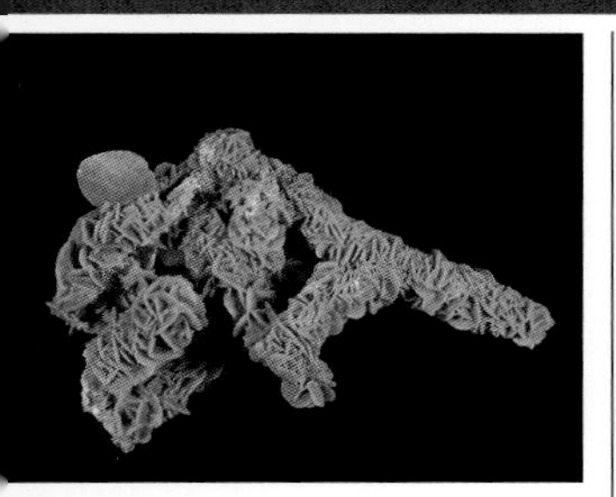

GYPSUM

Natural form: tabular crystals with curved faces; fibrous, massive, or granular.

Hardness: can be scratched with a finger nail.

Colour: colourless, white, or possibly yellow, grey, or brown if stained by impurities; white streak; glassy, pearly, or dull lustre.

Found: in areas where sea water has evaporated or as desert roses; widespread.

Uses: to make plaster of Paris, fertilizers.

I-SPY points: 10

Date: ______________

MALACHITE

Natural form: rounded banded masses, or as fibres.

Hardness: can be scratched with a knife.

Colour: bright green; pale-green streak; dull to silky sheen.

Found: associated with oxidized copper deposits, such as North Wales.

Uses: as a source of copper, jewellery, ornamental.

I-SPY points: 40

Date: ______________

BARYTE

Natural form: tabular, or as diamond- shaped prisms; fibrous, or as cockscomb masses.
Hardness: easily scratched by a knife.
Colour: colourless, white, or stained by impurities; white streak; glassy to pearly lustre.
Found: in veins associated with copper, zinc, iron and nickel; widespread.
Uses: in paint and textile industries; as a drilling mud in the oil industry; 'barium meal' in hospital investigations.

I-SPY points: 10

Date:

APATITE

Natural form: tabular or prism-shaped crystals.
Hardness: can be scratched with a knife.
Colour: green, yellow, white, brown, possibly tinged with red or blue; white streak; glassy lustre.
Found: in veins and in association with pegmatites, bedded phosphates, and in fossil bones; widespread.
Uses: to make fertilizers.

I-SPY points: 40

Date:

OLIVINE

Natural form: as grains in basalts or as poorly shaped masses.
Hardness: will scratch glass.
Colour: olive green, white, yellow-brown, or black.
Found: in rocks low in quartz, such as basalt and gabbro; widespread.
Uses: in the manufacture of high-temperature bricks; semi-precious stone (peridot).

I-SPY points: 30

Date: ____________

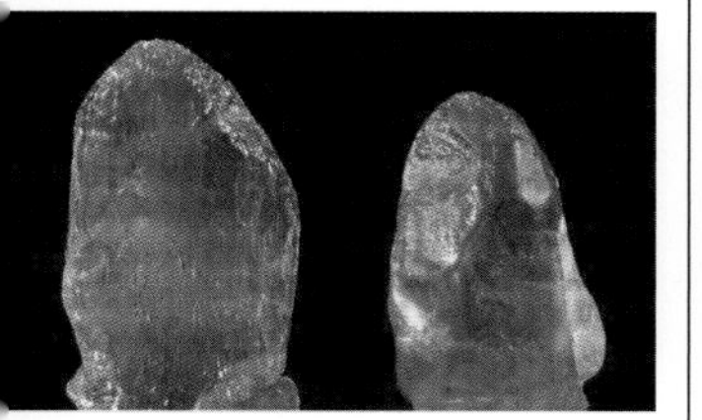

VANADINITE

Natural form: short or long prisms, needle-like, or globular.
Hardness: will scratch glass.
Colour: orange-red, brown-red, and yellow; white, yellow-white streak; glassy lustre.
Found: in association with lead minerals, sometimes in limestone; rare.
Uses: in the manufacture of steel.

I-SPY points: 50

Date: ____________

HORNBLENDE

Natural form: long or short prisms, or as granular or fibrous masses.

Hardness: will just scratch a knife blade.

Colour: shades of green to almost black; glassy lustre.

Found: in igneous rocks and some metamorphic rocks that have undergone change through medium grades of pressure and temperature; widespread.

Uses: identifying igneous rocks such as granite, syenite and diorite. Perfect crystals sought by collectors.

I-SPY points: 30

Date: ____________

ZIRCON

Natural form: prisms ending in double pyramids.

Hardness: will scratch glass.

Colour: brown, reddish brown, less commonly yellow, green, or violet; white streak; glassy lustre.

Found: in association with pegmatite veins and as a minor mineral in granites and syenites such as south-west England and Scotland.

Uses: gemstone.

I-SPY points: 40

Date: ____________

GARNET

Natural form: rhomb-like crystals or massive.
Hardness: will scratch glass.
Colour: varies with type, eg pyrope is deep red to black, uvarovite clear green; glassy or resin-like lustre.
Found: in association with schists, gneisses (almandine), serpentinites (pyrope), granites and pegmatites (spessartine) such as the Lake District and Scotland.
Uses: in abrasives and as gemstones.

I-SPY points: 20

Date: ____________

CHIASTOLITE

Natural form: prisms or crystals that are square in cross-section.
Hardness: will scratch glass.
Colour: usually pink or red, but brown, green, and grey forms have been found.
Found: in association with fine-grained metamorphic rocks and pegmatite veins; in Scotland, for example.
Uses: in spark plugs for the motor industry; clear green variety used as a gemstone.

I-SPY points: 15

Date: ____________

TOPAZ

Natural form: prisms or massive.
Hardness: almost as hard as diamond, will scratch glass.
Colour: usually pale yellow, blue, or less commonly green or pink.
Found: in quartz veins, granite pegmatites, or rhyolites; rare.
Uses: as a gemstone.

I-SPY points: 50

Date:

TOURMALINE

Natural form: long prisms with furrowed faces; triangular in cross-section.
Hardness: will scratch glass.
Colour: often black, but green, blue, brown, and pink varieties have been found.
Found: in granite pegmatites, gneisses, and schists; in south-west England, the Lake District and Scotland.
Uses: in the electrical industry and as a gemstone.

I-SPY points: 30

Date:

QUARTZ

Natural form: commonly as six-sided prisms; massive in veins.
Hardness: cannot be scratched with a knife.
Colour: usually colourless or white; semi-precious varieties are coloured, eg rose quartz, citrine, smoky quartz.
Found: abundant in many rocks; widespread.
Uses: quartz sand in the building industry, abrasives, semi-precious stones.

I-SPY points: 10

Date:

TALC

Natural form: granular or 'banded' masses; crystals uncommon.
Hardness: very soft.
Colour: white, pale green; white streak; soapy feel and dull lustre.
Found: in association with schists; widespread.
Uses: as talcum powder, filler, soapstone, and in the ceramics industries.

I-SPY points: 30

Date:

OPAL

Natural form: rounded, massive, stalactite-like forms, or as a replacement mineral. A form of quartz

Hardness: harder than a knife blade.

Colour: variable, colourless, milky white, red, brown, blue, green and black. Fire Opal shows a play of vivid colours.

Found: in association with hot springs and geysers; may fill cavities in rocks, formed at low temperatures; rare.

Uses: gemstone; one form used as an abrasive.

I-SPY points: 50

Date: ____________

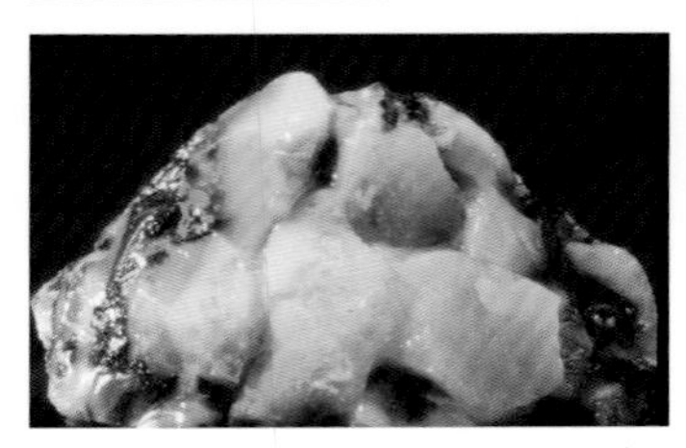

AGATE

Natural form: layered and banded in rings; often forms hollow nodules called geodes; it is a form of quartz.

Hardness: as quartz.

Colour: colourless to highly coloured.

Found: common in volcanic lavas as in Scotland.

Uses: ornamental and semi-precious stones.

I-SPY points: 40

Date: ____________

ORTHOCLASE FELDSPAR

Natural form: short, 'flattened' prisms.
Hardness: cannot be scratched with a knife.
Colour: white to pale pink; white streak; lustre pearly to glassy.
Found: abundant in granites, microgranites, and many other igneous and metamorphic rocks.
Uses: for making porcelain and its surface glass.

I-SPY points: 20

Date: ______________

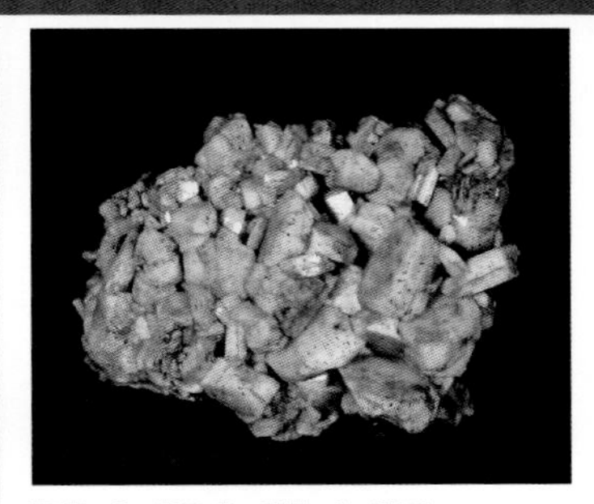

PLAGIOCLASE FELDSPAR

Natural form: prisms and as tabular crystals.
Hardness: as orthoclase.
Colour: white, less commonly pink or with green or brown.
Colour: white streak; lustre pearly to glassy.
Found: abundant in many igneous rocks; widespread.
Uses: in the ceramics industry.

I-SPY points: 20

Date: ______________

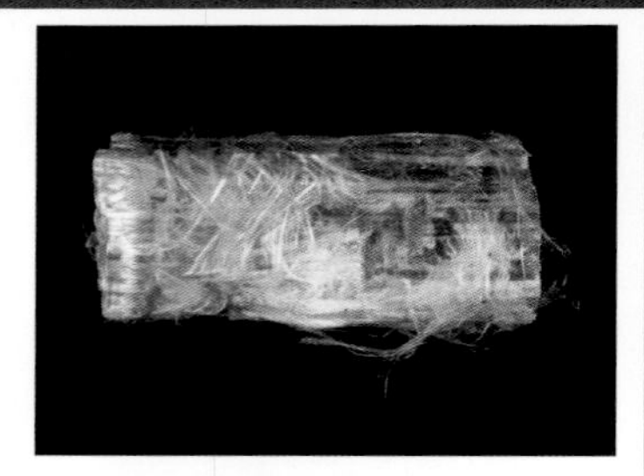

CHRYSOTILE (ASBESTOS)

Natural form: fibrous, platy, or layered.

Hardness: easily scratched with a knife.

Colour: white, yellow, various greens; colourless streak; waxy to pearly lustre.

Found: as a minor mineral in igneous rocks, notably in serpentinites as in Scotland.

Uses: fire protection.

I-SPY points: 40

Date:

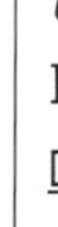

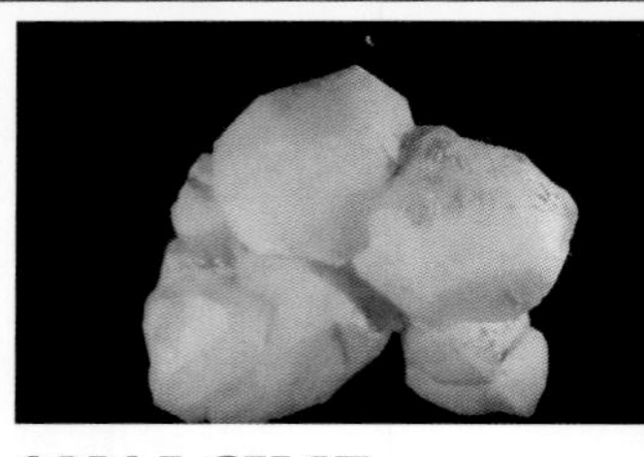

ANALCIME (ANALCITE)

Natural form: granular or massive.

Hardness: can just be scratched by a knife.

Colour: pink, white, grey, yellow, green; white streak; glassy lustre.

Found: south-west England, Scotland.

Uses: in chemical industries.

I-SPY points: 50

Date:

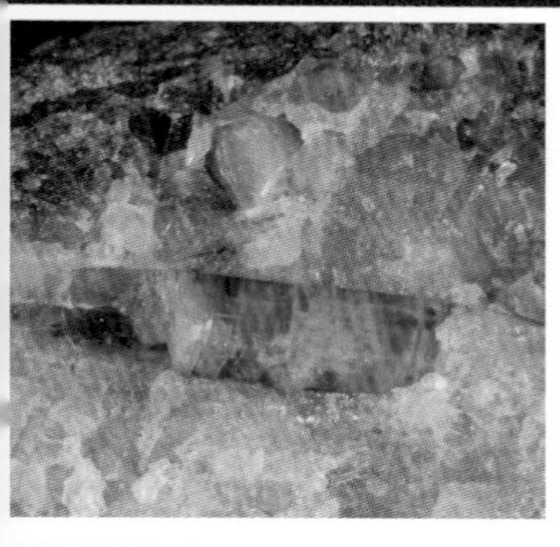

EMERALD

Natural form: as hexagonal prismatic crystals, sometime striated along their length.
Hardness: will scratch glass and knife.
Colour: pale to dark green. Transparent vivid green emeralds are prized by collectors.
Found: in granite cavernous pegmatites where they may form large crystals.
Uses: gemstone in jewellery. Emerald is a form of the mineral Beryl and a source of beryllium.

I-SPY points: 10

Date: ____________

TIGER'S EYE

Natural form: orange-yellowish-brown and fibrous quartz vein mineral replacing blue asbestos.
Hardness: easily scratched by topaz but with difficulty by a steel file.
Colour: pale orange-yellow.
Found: in metamorphic rocks such as schists and in well bedded ironstone deposits.
Uses: ornamental use in decorative jewellery

I-SPY points: 20

Date: ____________

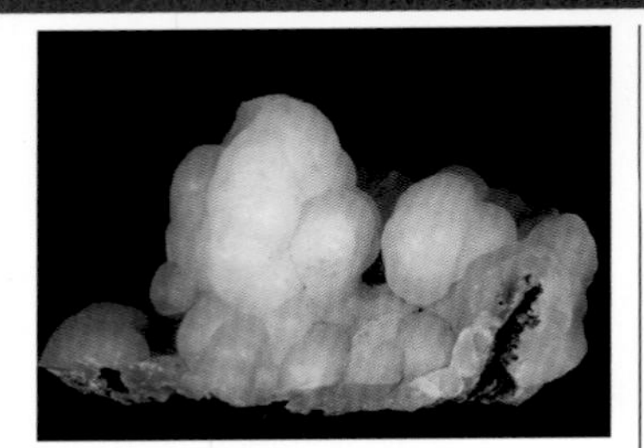

CHALCEDONY

Natural form: bulbous, kidney-shaped, stalactitic/stalagmitic. Often banded.
Hardness: scratches steel file, but not topaz.
Colour: variable from translucent to opaque white to red, brown, black.
Found: as veins and in cavity linings or fillings in various rocks; or as a replacement mineral.
Uses: jewellery and ornamental objects.

I-SPY points: 30

Date: ____________

LABRADORITE

Natural form: as tabular crystals, but also massive in igneous rocks such as larvikite where it is easily identified by its play of colours.
Hardness: scratched with difficulty by steel file, but easily by quartz.
Colour: white to dull grey, but easily identified by its play of blue and green colours.
Found: in igneous rocks, particularly abundant in the syenite Larvikite from Norway.
Uses: mineral collectors. Larvikite is used on the coast to replace less efficient timber breakwaters.

I-SPY points: 25

Date: ____________

Igneous rocks are those rocks that have crystallized out from magma (molten rock) as it has cooled.

GRANITE

Grain size: coarse to very coarse.
Colour: white, pink, or grey.
Texture: often with well-shaped crystals of feldspar; quartz, biotite, muscovite.
Found: often cross-cuts country rocks in areas of ancient rocks; south-west England, Scotland, the Lake District.
Uses: kerb stones, facing stone.

Which city in Scotland is known as 'the granite city'?

I-SPY points: 10, double with answer

Date: ____________

GRANITE PEGMATITE

Grain size: very coarse to gigantic.
Colour: uneven or patchy; mostly white, pink, or red.
Texture: large to huge crystals roughly parallel to one another.
Found: as cross-cutting dykes near granite intrusions; such as south-west England and Scotland.
Uses: mineral collectors paradise! Many contain gem minerals such as beryl, emerald, quartz, ruby, sapphire, topaz, tourmaline and zircon.

I-SPY points: 20

Date: ____________

MICROGRANITE

Grain size: individual crystals medium sized but larger, well-formed quartz and feldspar crystals may stand out.
Colour: speckled white, grey, pink.
Texture: may show flow features, with crystals parallel to one another.
Found: as intrusions or veins; south-west England, the Lake District, Scotland.
Uses: road stone, kerbstones.

I-SPY points: 10

Date: ____________

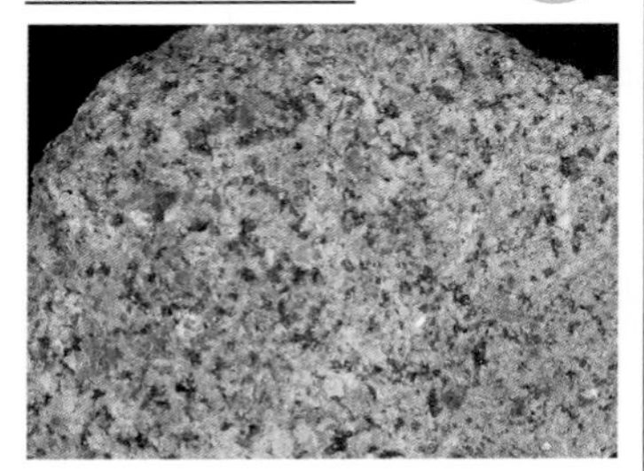

SYENITE

Grain size: coarse to very coarse.
Colour: similar to granites or slightly darker.
Texture: grains tend to be of equal size. Crystals are mostly feldspars with no more than 10% quartz.
Found: as cross-cutting dykes and as sills in Scotland.
Uses: ornamental. Polished slabs for facing buildings. Quarried as roadstone.

I-SPY points: 30

Date: ____________

ANDESITE

Grain size: fine to glassy.
Colour: green, brown, purple, grey, and almost black.
Texture: sometimes with larger crystals in the fine mass; may show flow features. Minerals include feldspars, hornblende, biotite, pyroxene.
Found: usually as lava flows; Lake District, Scotland.
Uses: building stone, decorative stone.

After which mountain range is this rock named?

I-SPY points: 20, double with answer

Date: ____________

DIORITE

Grain size: coarse, sometimes with large crystal growths.
Colour: speckled black and white, sometimes with a pink or green tinge.
Texture: equal grain size but large crystals may have developed.
Found: as individual intrusions; south-west England, North Wales, the Lake District, Scotland.
Uses: facing stone.

I-SPY points: 10

Date: ____________

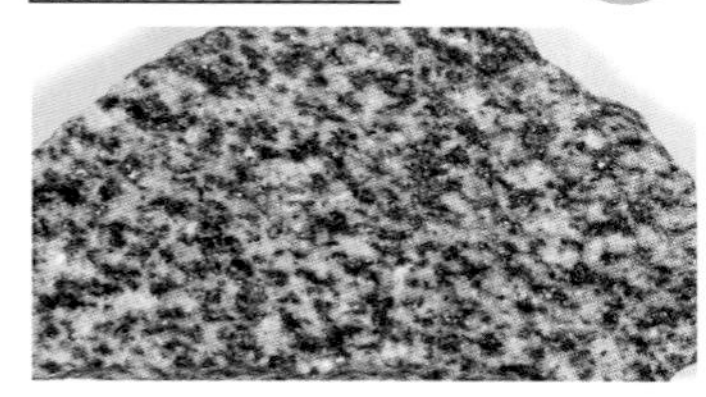

DOLERITE

Grain size: medium.
Colour: greyish- or greenish-black to black.
Texture: quite dense and moderately smooth to the touch. Minerals include quartz, feldspars, homblende, pyroxene, biotite, olivine, and magnetite.
Found: common in cross-cutting dykes and sills; south-west England, North Wales, Yorkshire, the Lake District and Scotland.
Uses: building and decorative stone.

I-SPY points: 10

Date:

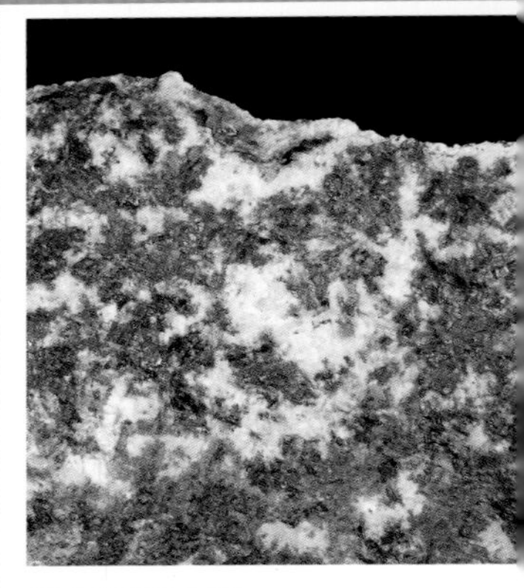

GABBRO

Grain size: coarse.
Colour: from grey to black but may have green and blue tinge.
Texture: grains obvious, often of equal size; rock may be layered with zones of light and dark minerals. Minerals mainly plagiociase feldspar, augite, olivine, or hornblende.
Found: in areas of ancient country rock as cross-cutting intrusions; south-west England, the Lake District, Scotland.
Uses: facing stone.

I-SPY points: 20

Date:

BASALT

Grain size: fine.
Colour: grey-black to black.
Texture: dense and relatively smooth to the touch; there may be small crystals of olivine in the fine mass. Minerals include feldspars, augite, olivine, and magnetite.
Found: the most common lava; occurs as flows which may cool to form columns; south-west England, North Wales, Yorkshire, the Lake District, Scotland.
Uses: building and decorative stone; memorial and gravestones.

I-SPY points: 10

Date: ____________

ROPY LAVA

Basaltic lavas may occur as volcanic flows or as widespread sheets. The top surface of the lava may look like rope (pahoehoe) or it may be rough, blocky, and cindery. Where the lava has been erupted into water, rounded, pillow-like structures are commonplace.
Found: North Wales, Scotland.
Uses: road stones, ornaments.

I-SPY points: 30, for any of pahoehoe or pillow lava

Date: ____________

OBSIDIAN

Natural form: opaque shiny black igneous rock showing curved conchoidal fracture. Translucent green on thin broken edges.

Grain Size: none – the rock is glassy.

Colour: black, brown or grey-black.

Texture: compact glass.

Found: as lava flow and edge of intrusive dykes where rapid cooling has taken place to form glass.

Uses: ancient cutting tools – knives, spear and arrow heads. Ornaments.

I-SPY points: 25

Date: ____________

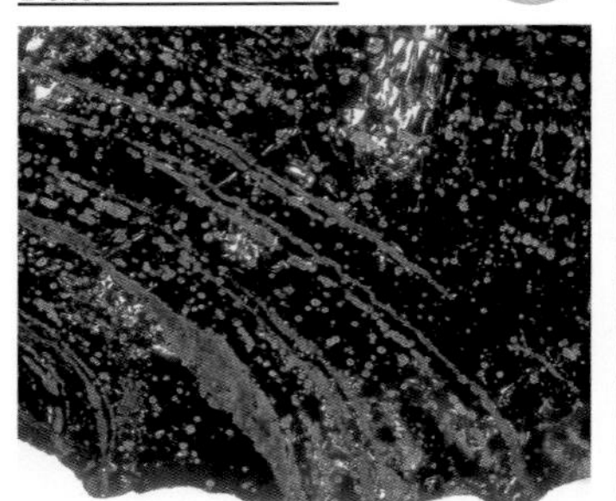

PITCHSTONE

Natural form: opaque dull black igneous rock showing poor curved surface fractures. Opaque on thin broken edges.

Grain Size: none – the rock is massive like "pitch".

Colour: black, brown or grey-black.

Texture: compact fine-grained volcanic rock.

Found: as lava flow and intrusive dykes where cooling has taken place to form finely crystalline opaque edge.

Uses: carved into ornaments.

I-SPY points: 25

Date: ____________

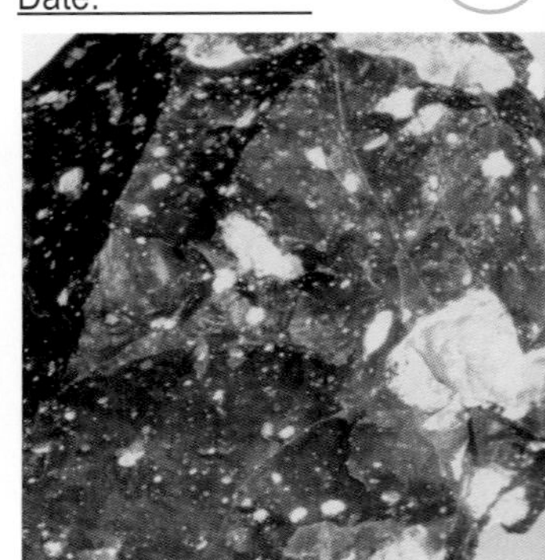

PUMICE

Grain size: fine.
Colour: white or off-white.
Texture: rough to the touch because of the high percentage of pores (vesicles) caused by escaping gas bubbles.
Found: associated with volcanoes and lava flows, and gas-rich layers; possibly in the Lake District and Westem Scotland.
Uses: as pumice-stone in the toiletries and cosmetics industries.

I-SPY points: 30

Date: ____________

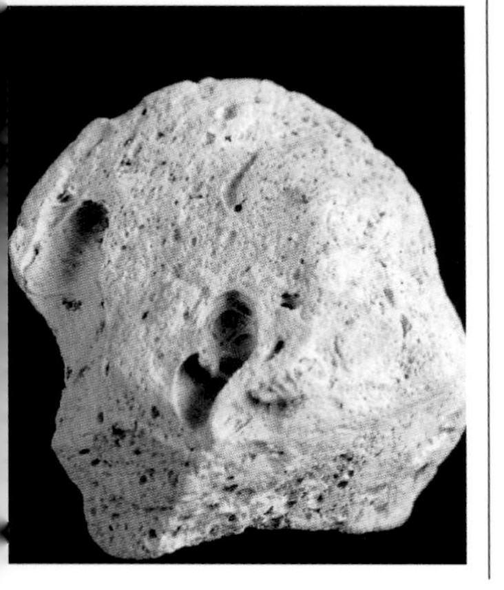

VOLCANIC ASH/ TUFF, VOLCANIC BOMBS

Explosive volcanoes produce clouds of rock fragments and dust. If this material remains loose, it is called an ash; if it is welded or consolidated, it is known as a tuff. Both may be layered or graded (ie coarse to fine). Fragments over 64mm in diameter that are elliptical or spindle-like in shape and have a 'bubble-rich' interior are known as bombs. It was the presence of volcanic ash in the atmosphere following an erupting volcano in Iceland that grounded planes in 2010.

I-SPY points: 20, for any one of ash, tuff or bomb

Date: ____________

Metamorphic Rocks

Rocks that have formed from other rocks that have been changed by heat, and or pressure, are known as metamorphic rocks.

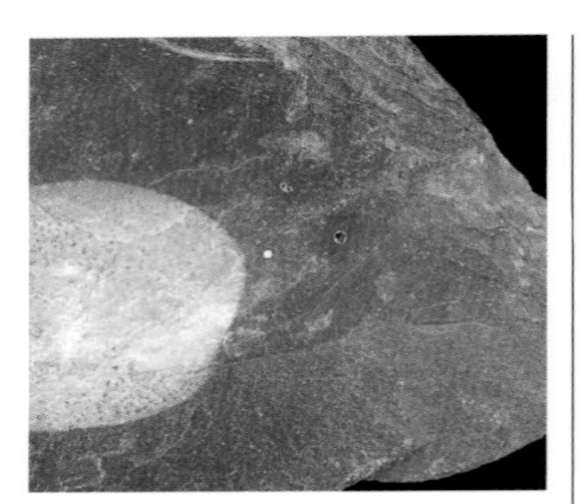

SLATE

Grain size: fine. Colour: green, grey, purple, or black.
Texture: even; the rock is smooth and splits easily into flat sheets; the mineral grains are so fine that it is difficult to identify them without the use of a microscope.
Found: in areas where rocks have undergone changes in pressure and temperature; south-west England, North Wales, the Lake District.
Uses: floor tiles, roofing slates, billiard tables, gravestones.

I-SPY points: 10

Date: ____________

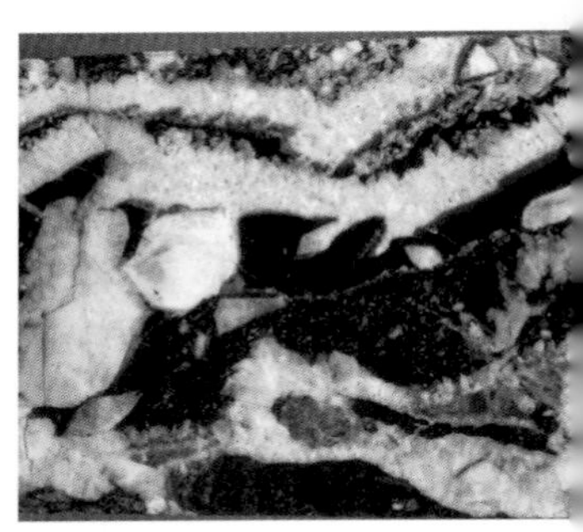

MARBLE

Grain size: medium to coarse.
Colour: white to grey with green, red, or black varieties known locally.
Texture: smooth to sugary; may be banded; fossils may be found in marbles that have been exposed to lower changes in temperature and pressure.
Found: areas of regional metamorphism; Scotland.
Uses: ideal building stone and decorative stone; it is often used by Sculptors.

I-SPY points: 30

Date: ____________

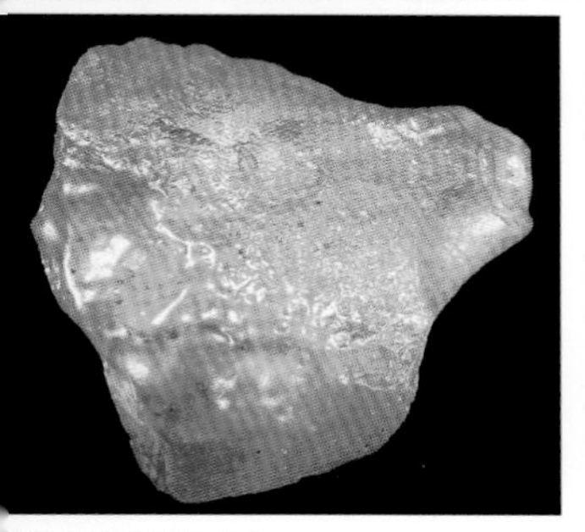

TEKTITE

Grain size: none – the rock is a glass. This specimen is 4.5 x 4.5cm and 55gms

Colour: translucent medium yellow with smooth 'puckered' surface

Texture: glassy-vitreous.

Found: Libyan desert. Formed by large meteorite strike generating sufficient heat to melt the surrounding sand and explosively distributing it over a large area around the impact site.

Uses: a rare rock much sought after by rock and mineral collectors.

I-SPY points: 30

Date: ____________

SERPENTINITE

Grain size: medium to coarse.

Colour: green, grey-green to black.

Texture: waxy appearance, sometimes with a splintery fracture. Minerals mainly olivine, hornblende, pyroxene, and mica.

Found: as cross-cutting intrusions. Serpentinites are formed mostly by the alteration of other rocks. In south-west England and Scotland.

Uses: ornaments and as facing stone.

I-SPY points: 20

Date: ____________

GNEISS

Grain size: medium to coarse.
Colour: speckled white, grey, or pink; streaked or layered with darker minerals.
Texture: rough to the touch, granular, may be layered or banded; the bands may be folded. Minerals include feldspar, quartz, muscovite, biotite, and hornblende.
Found: in areas that have undergone the highest grades of temperature and pressure changes; parts of south-west England and Scotland.
Uses: road stone, decorative stone.

I-SPY points: 30

Date: ____________

SCHIST

Grain size: fine to medium.
Colour: green, blue, grey, white, black, or brown.
Texture: smooth to rough to the touch; clearly defined layering of grains. Minerals include biotite, muscovite, quartz, feldspar, gamet, albite, staurolite.
Found: in areas where the rocks have been subjected to high-grade changes in pressure and temperature; south-west England North Wales, and Scotland.
Uses: road stone.

I-SPY points: 20

Date: ____________

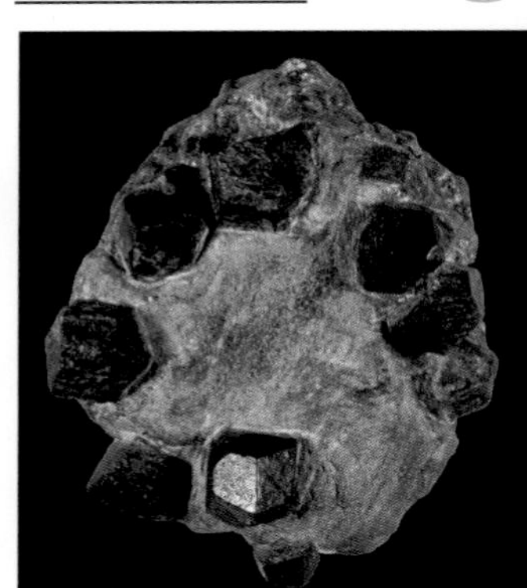

Rocks that have formed from the accumulation, burial, and hardening of mineral and rock fragments are known as sedimentary rocks.

CONGLOMERATE

Grain size: rounded pebbles greater than 2 mm in diameter.
Colour: variable.
Texture: coarse grained and poorly sorted; may be bound together. The pebbles may be mixed or of a single rock type. The rock may be held together (cemented) by calcite, silica, or iron minerals.
Found: in areas that were once criss-crossed by ancient streams or rivers or where the sea lapped against the shore (beach); widespread.
Uses: building stone and decorative stone.

I-SPY points: 10

Date:

BRECCIA

Grain size: greater than 2 mm.
Colour: variable.
Texture: coarse with angular fragments found in a fine to medium 'sandy' matrix; rarely, it may be bedded and layered.
Found: in areas that would once have been mountain slopes or below cliffs; widespread.
Uses: road stone, decorative stone.

I-SPY points: 20

Date:

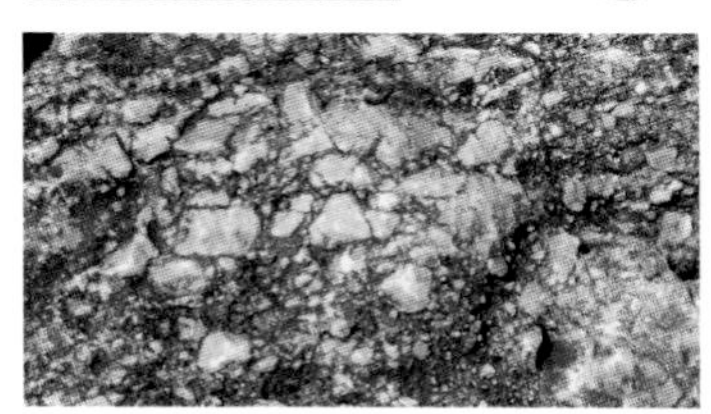

The word conglomerate has been adopted by corporations that form under one parent group.

SANDSTONE

Grain size: 2 mm in diameter-fine sandstone to grit.
Colour: variable. Texture: variable; grains may be angular or rounded; poor to well sorted; bedded; fossiliferous and characterized by ripple marks or burrows.
Found: in areas that were associated with rivers, lakes, or shallow seas; widespread.
Uses: in the building industry and in the manufacture of concrete.

I-SPY points: 10

Date: ____________

OOLITIC LIMESTONE

Grain size: mostly about 1 mm in diameter but may reach 2 mm.
Colour: white, yellow-brown.
Texture: oolitic limestones are composed of rounded spheres with each sphere built up in layers. The rock may contain a lot of fossils.
Found: in areas that once resembled the conditions found today in the shallow seas around the Bahamas; widespread especially in central England.
Uses: building stone.

What does the word 'oolitic' mean?

I-SPY points: 30, double with answer

Date: ____________

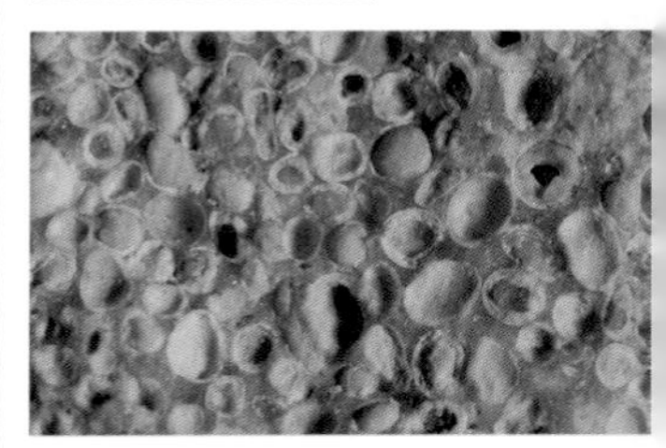

SHELLY LIMESTONE/ FOSSILIFEROUS LIMESTONE

Grain size: variable.
Colour: white, grey, buff, blue.
Texture: often coarse and poorly sorted; rich in mud or cemented by calcite.
Found: in areas where rocks were laid down in shallow sea water; widespread.
Uses: building and decorative stone; even when cut and polished fossils can be seen.

I-SPY points: 10

Date: ___________

CHALK

Grain size: fine to very fine.
Colour: white and grey; rarely red or yellow.
Texture: porous and crumbly; often contains nodules of flint. Chalk is a pure limestone made up of the skeletons of microscopic sea creatures.
Found: in areas once covered by deep, widespread seas during a period of Earth's history called the Upper Cretaceous (100-70 million years ago); southern and eastern England.
Uses: road fill, lime, building stone, cement manufacture.

I-SPY points:10

Date: ___________

IRONSTONE

Grain size: fine to coarse; may be banded, bedded, and oolitic.
Colour: yellow, green, brown, or red.
Texture: sometimes nodular; grains may be cemented together with calcite.
Found: associated with other sediments such as the English Midlands.
Uses: as a source of iron ore.

I-SPY points: 20

Date:

FLINT NODULE (CHERT NODULE)

Grain size: fine to very fine.
Colour: brown, brown-black, black, bluish when fresh; outside coated white.
Texture: smooth and glassy with a rounded conchoidal fracture; splinters easily.
Found: in chalk and other limestones.
Uses: to make walls and in buildings.

To what use did primitive humans put flint?

I-SPY points: 20, double with answer

Date:

PYRITE (MARCASITE) NODULE

Grain size: long, needle-like crystals.

Colour: dull yellow, bronze.

Texture: rough and dull on the outside; bright radiating crystals inside the nodule.

Found: in chalk areas, particularly, as rounded, cylinder-shaped, or shapeless nodules in chalks, shales and mudstones.

Uses: little except ornamental.

I-SPY points: 30

Date: ____________

METEORITE

Grain size: fine to coarse.

Colour: variable, speckled to dark grey in stony meteorites; iron meteorites bronzy yellow to grey.

Texture: often with a definite outer coat or crust; iron meteorites may have a pitted surface.

Found: in open areas; rare.

Uses: museum specimens.

What is the common name often given to a small meteorite that burns up before reaching Earth?

I-SPY points: 40, double with answer

Date: ____________

CALAMITES

Age: Upper Carboniferous 300-286 mya.
Form: jointed stem of horsetail (living Equisetum is a garden weed); shoots may arise from joints; stem is often ridged.
Found: in coal measure sandstones and shales; Wales, Yorkshire, and Scotland.
Size: individual plants reached heights of 40 m.

I-SPY points: 30

Date: ______________

NEUROPTERIS

Age: Upper Carboniferous 300-286 mya.
Form: fern-like leaf or frond with many round 'leaflets' that have prominent veins along the midlines.
Found: in coals and coal measure mudstones and sandstones; Wales, Yorkshire, and Scotland.
Size: 5-8 cm across frond.

I-SPY points: 30

Date: ______________

Fossil: From Latin Fossus, literally having been dug up. These are the preserved remains or traces of animals, plants or other organisms found in rocks.

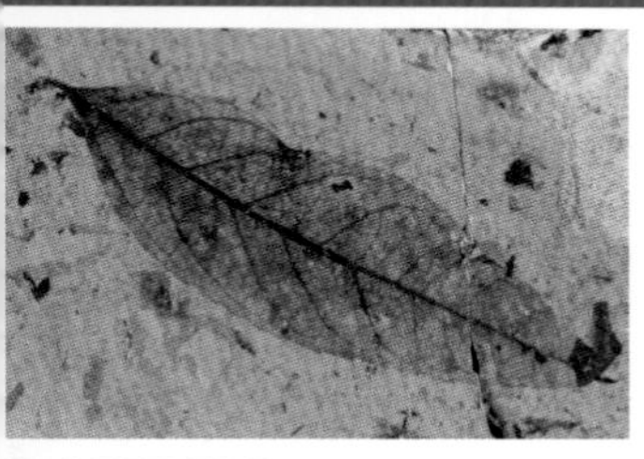

LAURUS

Age: Cretaceous-Recent 130 mya to present day.
Form: rather narrow leaf with undivided border; veins move outwards and up leaf from central vein.
Found: in fine-grained sediments, including chalk; southern England.
Size: 10-12 cm long.

I-SPY points: 40

Date: ____________

ANNULARIA

Age: Upper Carboniferous 300-286 mya.
Form: thin jointed stem with circlets of leaves; related to Calamites; leaves often found covering flat rock surfaces.
Found: in coal measure mudstones and shales; Wales, Yorkshire, and Scotland.
Size: 5-8 cm in diameter.

I-SPY points: 30

Date: ____________

NIPA (NIPADITES)

Age: Eocene-Recent 55 mya to present day.
Form: large oval-shaped seed, tapers towards tip; often appears ribbed.
Found: in Eocene clays associated with bored wood, such as around the Isle of Sheppey.
Size: 5-20 cm in height.

I-SPY points: 40

Date: ____________

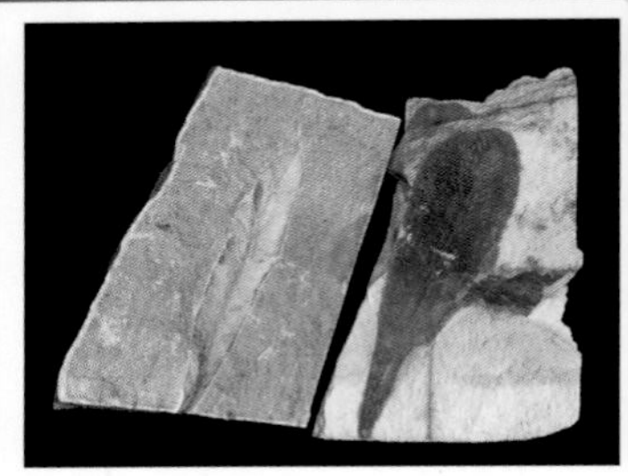

GLOSSOPTERIS

Age: Upper Carboniferous to Lower Permian. 300 – 200 mya.
Form: distinct leaf of seed fern, as illustrated.
Found: on flat bedding plane surfaces of mudstones and shales.
Size: illustrated specimens are 5 to 6 cm in length.

I-SPY points: 35

Date: ____________

Fossils can be found almost anywhere. Keep you eyes open if you are digging in the garden, you may be surprised what you can unearth.

CANINIA

Age: Lower Carboniferous 360-320 mya.
Form: large solitary coral with prominent septa (divisions), and many small, plate-like structures arranged in a circular manner inside the inner wall; long, cylindrical, often curved.
Found: in limestones and muddy limestones; Wales, the Midlands, Yorkshire, Scotland.
Size: 10-30 cm long.

I-SPY points: 20

Date:

ZAPHRENTIS

Age: Lower Carboniferous 360 - 320 mya.
Form: individual corals as slightly curved inverted cones.
Found: in Lower Carboniferous Reef Limestones, Visean Stage. UK.
Size: single corals up to 2.5 to 4.0 cm.

I-SPY points: 30

Date:

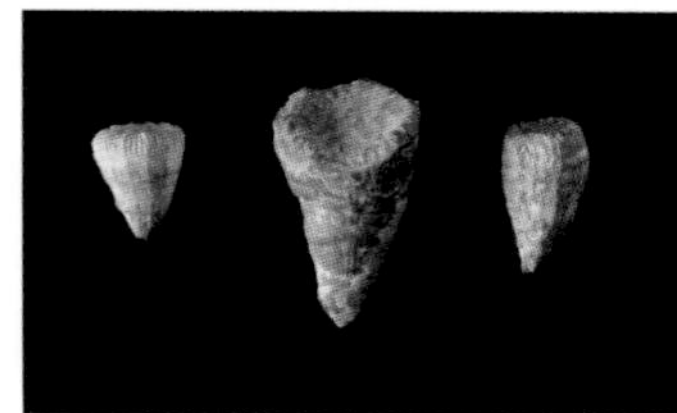

VENTRICULITES

Age: Cretaceous 145-65 mya.
Form: vase shaped with many pores in thin outer wall; wall appears grooved or slightly ribbed.
Found: in chalky limestones as individual fossils, sometimes replaced by chert; south-east England and Yorkshire.
Size: 5-8 cm in diameter.

I-SPY points: 30

Date: ____________

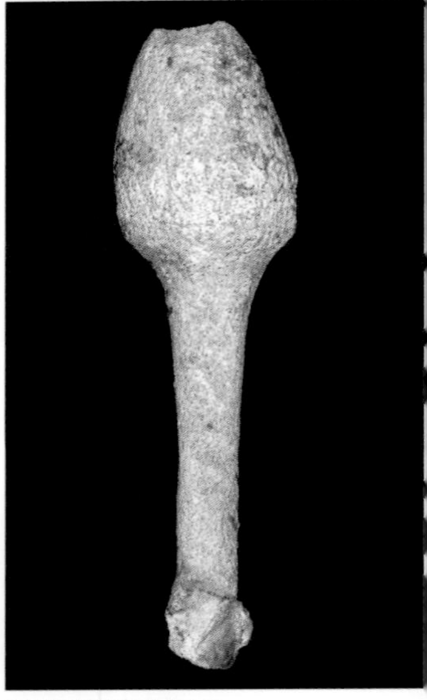

SIPHONIA

Age: Middle Cretaceous to Tertiary. 110-0.01 mya
Form: truncated pear-shaped club on long stalk.
Found: cretaceous chalk and later deposits.
Size: complete specimens up to 20 cm in length.

I-SPY points: 45

Date: ____________

Fossil Polyzoans

Polyzoans are sea animals that live in colonies that resemble moss.

LUNULITES

Age: Cretaceous-Eocene 144-55 mya.

Form: small, disc-like or cone-shaped colonies with pore-like openings arranged in distinct rows.

Found: in chalky limestones; southern England.

Size: 1-3 mm in diameter.

I-SPY points: 50

Date: ____________

FENESTELLA

Age: Ordovician-Permian 500-245 mya.

Form: delicate lace-like or net-like skeleton; pores appear in pairs on longer, radiating branches.

Found: in fine-grained mudstones and limestones such as in Wales.

Size: colonies 5-10 cm across.

I-SPY points: 40

Date: ____________

Fossil Brachiopods

mya = million years ago

Brachiopods are sea creatures that are protected by a hinged pair of shells (valves) similar to that of a cockle, for example. They are also known as 'lamp shells'.

SPIRIFER

Age: Carboniferous 360-285 mya. Spiriferids as a group lived Silurian-Permian.
Form: clam-like shell in two valves; hinge between valves long and straight; both valves usually ribbed; internal spiral skeleton.
Found: in limestones and muddy limestones; south-west England.
Size: 3-8 cm in width across the hinge.

I-SPY points: 40

Date: ____________

PRODUCTID

Age: Carboniferous 360-320 mya
Form: medium to very large with two valves of different sizes; larger valve strongly curved, smaller flat; both valves ribbed with strong ornament.
Found: limestones and muddy limestones; south-west England, Wales, the Midlands, Yorkshire, Scotland.
Size: 3- 20 cm.

I-SPY points: 20

Date: ____________

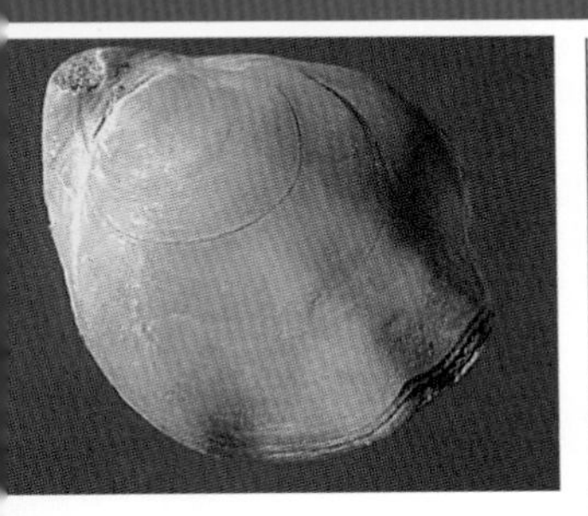

SELLATHYRIS

Age: Cretaceous 144-100 mya.
Form: medium-sized, smooth, two-valved shell; well-formed circular opening at top of larger valve; peardrop shaped, front edge strongly folded.
Found: in sandstones and shales; Isle of Wight.
Size: 2-3 cm long.

I-SPY points: 30

Date: ____________

RHYNCHONELLID

Age: Jurassic-Cretaceous 208-70 mya.
Form: strongly ribbed two-valve shell, with the valves roughly equal in size; the larger valve has a strongly beak-like development; small to medium sized.
Found: in limestones, muddy lime-stones, and sandstones; the English Midlands.
Size: 1-3 cm wide.

I-SPY points: 20

Date: ____________

Bivalves are mussel-like molluscs that lived in the sea.

VENERICARDIA

Age: Eocene 55-45 mya.
Form: medium- to large-size clam with two equal valves; there are two strong teeth along the internal hinge line; strong flattened ridges and lines ornament the outer surfaces.
Found: in sandy mudstones and claystones; south-east England.
Size: 5-10 cm wide.

I-SPY points: 30

Date: ____________

GRYPHEA

Age: Jurassic 245-208 mya.
Form: so-called 'devil's toenail'; two valves of very different sizes; lower one is large and strongly curved; smaller one acts as a lid; strong growth lines on larger valve.
Found: in shales and muddy limestones; Dorset and the English Midlands.
Size: 4-10 cm.

I-SPY points: 20

Date: ____________

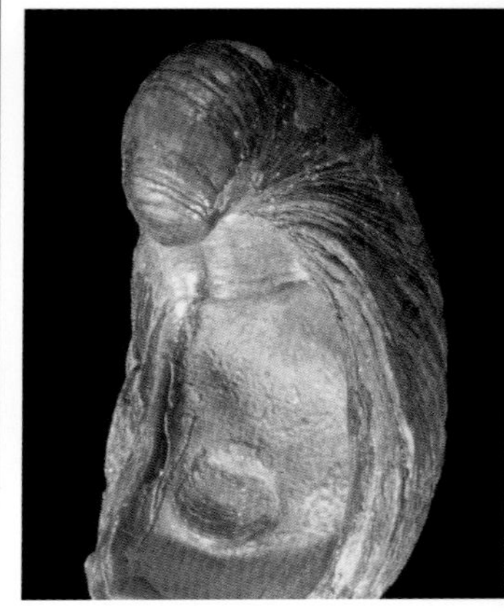

GLYCIMERIS

Age: Cretaceous-Recent 144 mya to present day.
Form: small to medium-sized clam with oval shape; valves have many teeth on curved hinge line; strong muscle scars on insides of valves; outer surface has a weak ornament of growth lines.
Found: in sands and shaly sandstones; East Anglia.
Size: 3-6 cm wide.

I-SPY points: 20

Date: ____________

MYOPHORA (TRIGONIA)

Age: Jurassic-Lower Cretaceous 208-120 mya.
Form: medium-sized clam with equal-sized valves; triangular outline with strong, flatter ridge surface in front of strongly ribbed area.
Found: in limestones, sandy limestones, shaly limestones; Dorset and the Midlands
Size: 3-8 cm wide.

I-SPY points: 20

Date: ____________

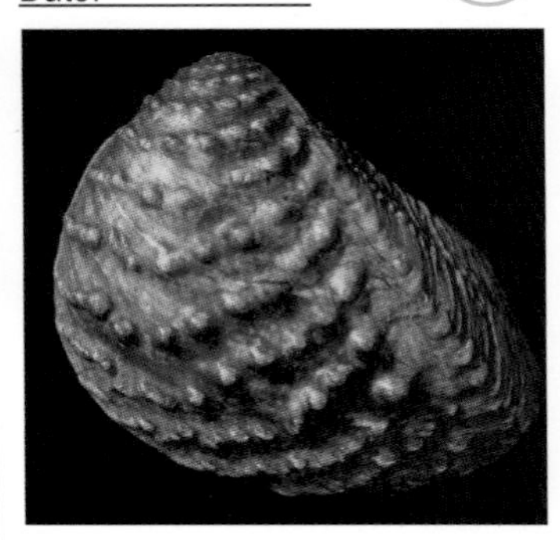

Gastropods are winkle-like molluscs.

BELLEROPHON

Age: Silurian-Permian 460-286 mya.
Form: coiled, wide shell which broadens towards the opening; strong ridge around middle, faintly ribbed by growth lines.
Found: muddy limestones and limestones; Wales.
Size: 5 cm across the opening.

I-SPY points: 40

Date:

TURRITELLA

Age: Cretaceous-Recent 144 mya-present day.
Form: long, high-spired shell made up of many whorls which are ornamented with spiral ribs; the opening is oval and simple.
Found: in sandstones, shales, and limestones; southem England.
Size: 3-15 cm long.

I-SPY points: 20

Date:

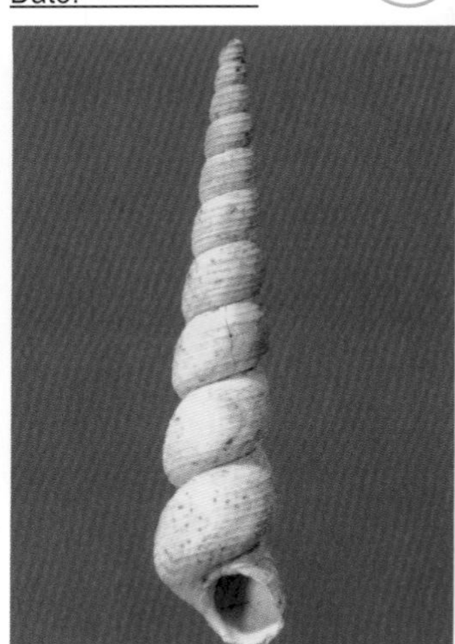

NEPTUNA

Age: Pleistocene 20 mya-0.01 mya.
Form: short coiled spiral shell tapering to apex. This specimen is unusual in that the coils are reversed with the body cavity opening on the left instead of the right. Hence the name Neptunia contraria.
Found: Red Crag deposits, Walton-on-Naze, Suffolk.
Size: 5-6 cm long.

I-SPY points: 30

Date:

NATICA

Age: Triassic-Recent 245 mya-present day.
Form: coiled medium-sized shell with a broad conical appearance; small, low spire; the opening has a thicker inner lip and is oval or rounded; smooth except for growth lines.
Found: in sands, sandstones, shales; southern England.
Size: 0.5-3 cm.

I-SPY points: 30

Date:

Whorls: a type of spiral or circular pattern.

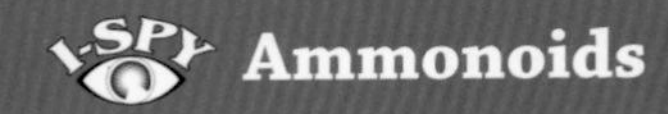

Ammonoids

mya = million years ago

Ammonoids are an extinct group of sea-dwelling molluscs with coiled shells resembling Catherine Wheels.

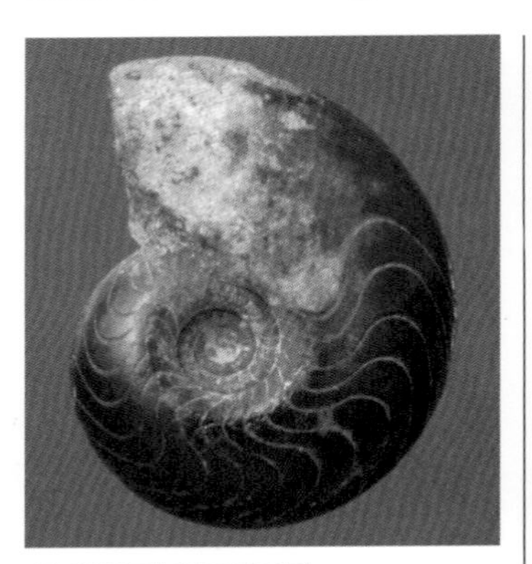

GONIATITE

Age: Carboniferous 360-286 mya.
Form: coiled shell with outer shell or whorl overlapping others; rounded and rather inflated appearance with simple sutures (divisions) between chambers.
Found: limestones and shales; Wales, Yorkshire, and Scotland.
Size: 3-6 cm in diameter.

I-SPY points: 30

Date:

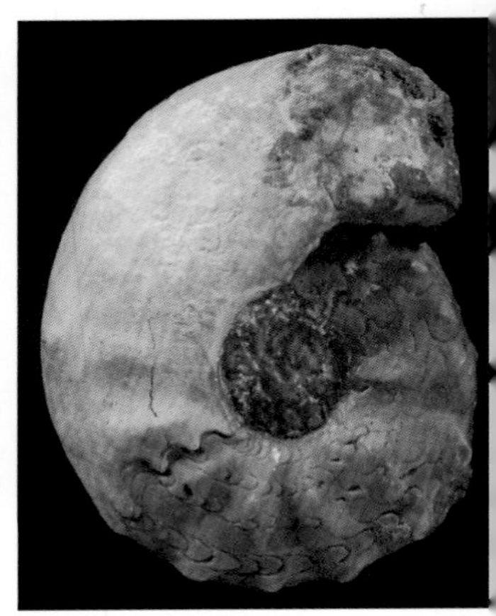

CERATITES

Age: Triassic 245-208 mya.
Form: coiled shell with slightly overlapping whorls; strongly ornamented with ribs and nodes; the sutures between chambers are folded into lobes and saddles.
Found: in limestones; rare.
Size: 5-12 cm in diameter.

I-SPY points: 50

Date:

DACTYLIOCERAS

Age: Lower Jurassic 208-180 mya.
Form: coiled shell with open appearance of whorls; slightly flattened side on, with regular strongs ribs that split into two over outer edge.
Found: muddy limestones, limestones, shales; Yorkshire.
Size: 5-10 cm in diameter.

I-SPY points: 30

Date: ____________

ARNIOCERAS

Age: Lower Jurassic. 178-155 mya.
Form: coiled ammonite with distinctive ribs and white wavy sutures.
Found: in mudstones and shales in Lower Liassic of Lower Jurassic.
Size: 4.5-5 cm diameter.

I-SPY points: 35

Date: ____________

HOPLITES

Age: Lower Cretaceous 144-125 mya.

Form: flattened or compressed shell, coiled with outer whorl overlapping inner ones; strongly ribbed and with raised bumps; the ribs are not continuous over the outer margin.

Found: clays and shales; the area of Folkestone, Kent.

Size: 2-10 cm in diameter.

I-SPY points: 20

Date: ____________

HAMITES

Age: Cretaceous 144-70 mya.

Form: uncoiled shell which curves and broadens towards the opening; curves are sharp and the shell is noted for the strong ribs that form complete circles around it.

Found: shales and mudstones; southern England.

Size: 10-20 cm long.

I-SPY points: 30

Date: ____________

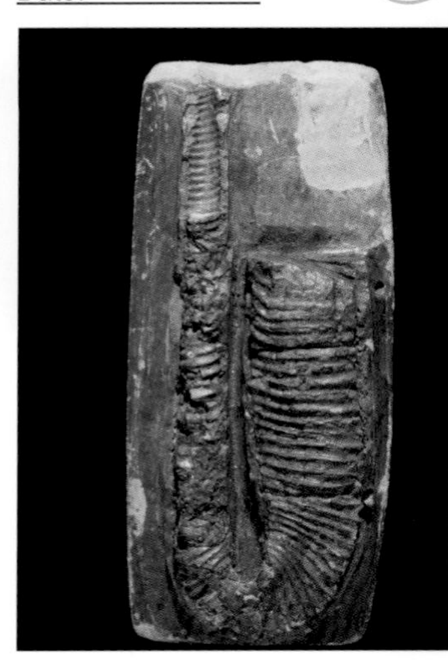

Belemnoids/Graptolites

Belemnoids are an extinct group of molluscs related to squids that lived in the sea. Fossils are bullet-like structures that once formed internal supports for the animals. Graptolites are an extinct group of sea creatures that lived together in colonies.

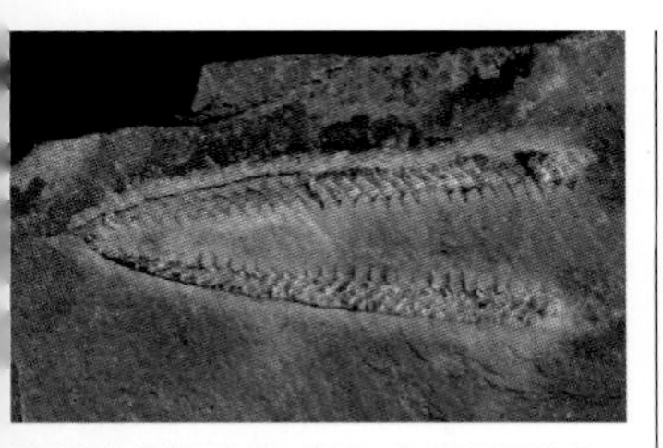

DIDYMOGRAPTUS

Age: Lower and Middle Ordovician 500-450 mya.
Form: so-called 'tuning-fork graptolite'; two well-formed branches with toothed inner edges; branches may also be horizontal in position.
Found: black shales; Wales, the Lake District, Scotland.
Size: 2-4 cm long.

How do graptolites get their name?

I-SPY points: 40, double with answer

Date:

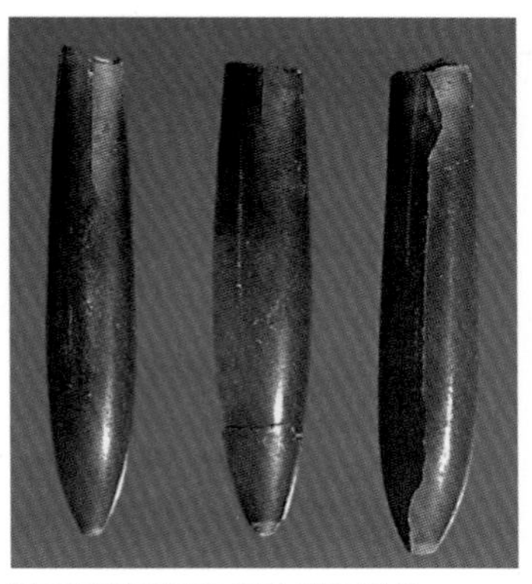

NEOHIBOLITES

Age: Upper Cretaceous 100-70 mya.
Form: bullet-shaped shell or guard; rounded in section with radiating fibres and growth lines prominent in broken cross-sections.
Found: shales and mudstones; southern England.
Size: 5-10 cm long.

I-SPY points: 40

Date:

I-SPY Echinoderms/Crinoids

mya = million years ago

Echinoderms are a group of creatures that includes sea lilies (crinoids), starfishes, and sea urchins (echinoids).

PENTACRINITES (PENTACRINUS)

Age: Triassic-Cretaceous 245-70 mya.

Form: large crinoid with long branched arms; stem and arms are made up of individual plates, called ossicles; stem ossicles are star shaped in cross-section.

Found: shales and muddy limestones; southern England.

Size: 20-40 cm tall.

I-SPY points: 30

Date: ____________

MICRASTER

Age: Upper Cretaceous 100-70 mya.

Form: heart-shaped sea urchin with mouth on the underside of test and the anus at the rear; small raised knobs occur as ornamentation.

Found: chalks and other limestones; southern England.

Size: 5-6 cm long.

I-SPY points: 20

Date: ____________

CONULUS

Age: Upper Cretaceous. 100-66 mya

Form: distinct conical test (shell) with small tubercules projecting from surface.

Found: in Upper Cretaceous Chalk.

Size: 4 cm in height.

I-SPY points: 35

Date: __________

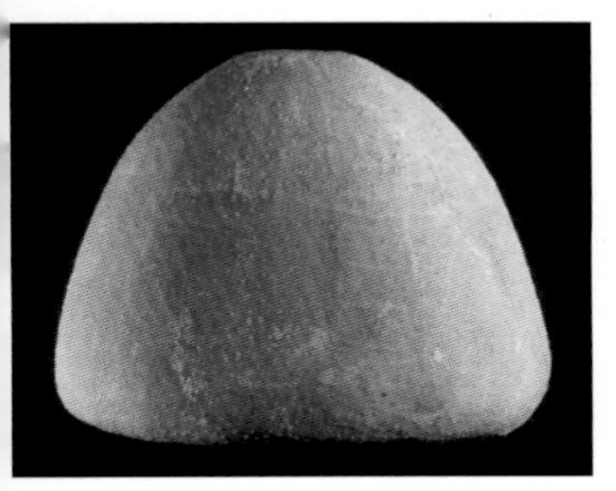

HEMICIDARIS

Age: Jurassic-Upper Cretaceous 208-70 mya.

Form: medium-sized rounded skeleton (test) with obvious radial symmetry; strongly ornamented, with large bosses to receive spines.

Found: limestones and chalky limestones; southern England, the English Midlands.

Size: 2-4 cm in diameter.

I-SPY points: 30

Date: __________

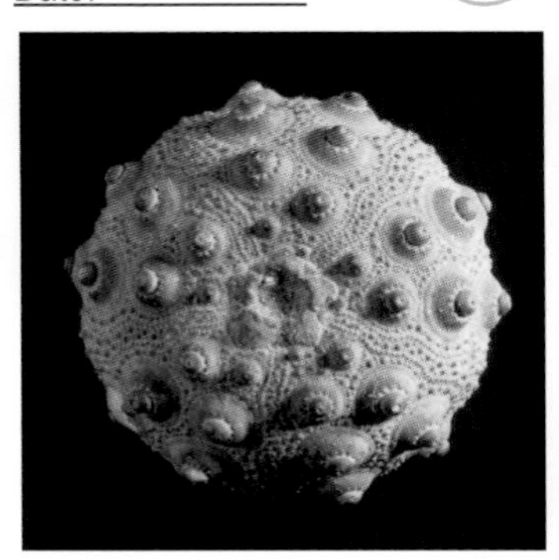

mya = million years ago

Trilobites are an extinct group of sea creatures related to insects.

CALYMENE

Age: Silurian-Devonian 435-360 mya.

Form: medium-sized with many body segments and short, rounded tail; headshield has small eyes and a distinctive central area; there are short spines on the sides of the headshield.

Found: limestones and muddy limestones; the Lake District, Scotland.

Size: 10 cm long.

I-SPY points: 40

Date: ____________

DALMANITES

Age: Silurian to Lower Devonian. 420-380 mya.

Form: segmented body with pointed tail, lateral spines and rounded head.

Found: on shale bedding planes.

Size: Up to 5 cm.

I-SPY points: 35

Date: ____________

ONNIA (TRINUCLEID)

Age: Ordovician 500-435 mya.
Form: small to medium with broad headshield, extended into long spines; body and tail short with few segments; front of headshield strongly pitted.
Found: mudstones and shales; Wales.
Size: 3 cm long.

I-SPY points: 30

Date: ____________

INSECT IN AMBER

Age: common in Oligocene 38-26 mya.
Form: various insects and spiders found trapped in resin of firs and pines; often sold as jewellery.
Found: sands and sandstones; rare.
Size: variable.

I-SPY points: 50

Date: ____________

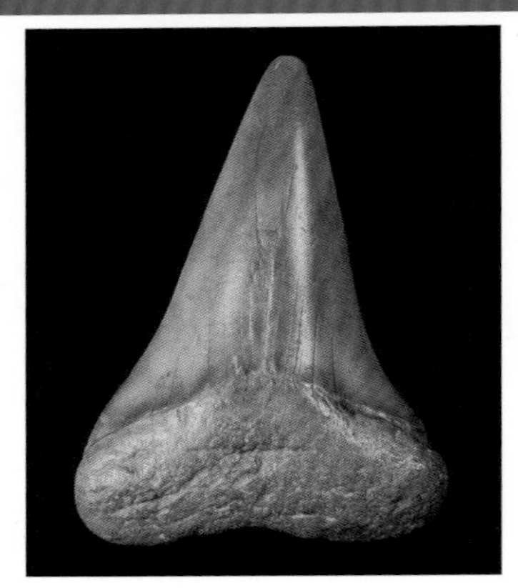

LAMNA

Age: Cretaceous-Pliocene 144-2 mya.
Form: robust shark's tooth, medium sized with two smaller points on the sides of central, larger tooth structure; strong, rough-textured 'root'.
Found: sandstones and silty shales; southern England.
Size: 2-4 cm.

I-SPY points: 30

Date: ____________

GOSIUTICHTHYS (BONY FISH)

Age: Cretaceous-Eocene. 135-Present. Specimen is 40 mya old.
Form: bony fish are similar to the specimen illustrated with variations according to species.
Found: on flat bedding planes of mudstones and shales.
Size: Generally 6-10 cm in length, but larger specimens do occur.

I-SPY points: 35

Date: ____________

Index

First published by Michelin Maps and Guides 2012 © Michelin, Proprietaires-Editeurs 2012. Michelin and the Michelin Man are registered Trademarks of Michelin. Created and produced by Blue Sky Publishing Limited. All rights reserved. No part of this publication may be reproduced, copied or transmitted in any form without the prior consent of the publisher. Print services by FingerPrint International Book production – fingerprint@pandora.be. The publisher gratefully acknowledges the contribution of the I-Spy team: Camilla Lovell, Geoff Watts and Ruth Neilson in the production of this title; The publisher gratefully acknowledges Dr Basil Booth for all of the text and technical assistance; GeoScience Features Picture Library who provided all the photographs in this book. All logos, images, designs and image rights are © the copyright holders and are used with kind thanks and permission.

10 9 8 7 6 5 4 3 2 1

Answers: P4: Pyrite – Fool's Gold, **P4:** Graphite- Lead, **P12:** Dolomite Mountains – Northern Italy, **P27:** Granite – Aberdeen, **P29:** Andesite – the Andes Mountains, **P38:** Oolitic – egg-like because the individual grains resemble fish eggs, **P40:** Flint – to make stone tools and weapons, **P41:** Meteorite – Shooting/falling star, **P57:** Didymograptus – from the Greek word graphos meaning writing; graptolites resemble strange writing in stone.

HOW TO GET YOUR I-SPY CERTIFICATE AND BADGE

Every time you score 1000 points or more in an I-Spy book, you can apply for a certificate

HERE'S WHAT TO DO, STEP BY STEP:

Certificate

- Ask an adult to check your score
- Ask his or her permission to apply for a certificate
- Apply online to www.ispymichelin.com
- Enter your name and address and the completed title
- We will send you back via e mail your certificate for the title

Badge

- Each I-Spy title has a cut out (page corner) token at the back of the book
- Collect five tokens from different I-Spy titles
- Put Second Class Stamps on two strong envelopes
- Write your own address on one envelope and put a £1 coin inside it (for protection). Fold, but do not seal the envelope, and place it inside the second envelope
- Write the following address on the second envelope, seal it carefully and post to:

I-Spy Books
Michelin Maps and Guides
Hannay House
39 Clarendon Road
Watford
WD17 1JA